HAL•LEONARD® BASS PLAY-ALONG

AUDIO ACCESS INCLUDED

2nd Edition

VOL. 4

'90s ROCK

PLAYBACK+
Speed • Pitch • Balance • Loop

To access audio visit:
www.halleonard.com/mylibrary

"Enter Code"
8176-0108-0851-2073

ISBN 978-1-5400-5491-3

HAL•LEONARD®

Visit Hal Leonard Online at
www.halleonard.com

Contact us:
Hal Leonard
7777 West Bluemound Road
Milwaukee, WI 53213
Email: info@halleonard.com

In Europe, contact:
Hal Leonard Europe Limited
42 Wigmore Street
Marylebone, London, W1U 2RN
Email: info@halleonardeurope.com

In Australia, contact:
Hal Leonard Australia Pty. Ltd.
4 Lentara Court
Cheltenham, Victoria, 3192 Australia
Email: info@halleonard.com.au

CONTENTS

BASS NOTATION LEGEND

Bass music can be notated two different ways: on a *musical staff*, and in *tablature*

THE MUSICAL STAFF shows pitches and rhythms and is divided by bar lines into measures. Pitches are named after the first seven letters of the alphabet.

TABLATURE graphically represents the bass fingerboard. Each horizontal line represents a string, and each number represents a fret.

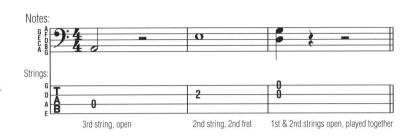

3rd string, open   2nd string, 2nd fret   1st & 2nd strings open, played together

HAMMER-ON: Strike the first (lower) note with one finger, then sound the higher note (on the same string) with another finger by fretting it without picking.

PULL-OFF: Place both fingers on the notes to be sounded. Strike the first note and without picking, pull the finger off to sound the second (lower) note.

LEGATO SLIDE: Strike the first note and then slide the same fret-hand finger up or down to the second note. The second note is not struck.

SHIFT SLIDE: Same as legato slide, except the second note is struck.

TRILL: Very rapidly alternate between the notes indicated by continuously hammering on and pulling off.

TREMOLO PICKING: The note is picked as rapidly and continuously as possible.

VIBRATO: The string is vibrated by rapidly bending and releasing the note with the fretting hand.

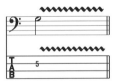

SHAKE: Using one finger, rapidly alternate between two notes on one string by sliding either a half-step above or below.

NATURAL HARMONIC: Strike the note while the fret hand lightly touches the string directly over the fret indicated.

MUFFLED STRINGS: A percussive sound is produced by laying the fret hand across the string(s) without depressing them and striking them with the pick hand.

BEND: Strike the note and bend up the interval shown.

BEND AND RELEASE: Strike the note and bend up as indicated, then release back to the original note. Only the first note is struck.

RIGHT-HAND TAP: Hammer ("tap") the fret indicated with the "pick-hand" index or middle finger and pull off to the note fretted by the fret hand.

LEFT-HAND TAP: Hammer ("tap") the fret indicated with the "fret-hand" index or middle finger.

SLAP: Strike ("slap") string with right-hand thumb.

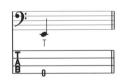

POP: Snap ("pop") string with right-hand index or middle finger.

Additional Musical Definitions

   (accent)   • Accentuate note (play it louder)

   (accent)   • Accentuate note with great intensity

   (staccato)   • Play the note short

D.S. al Coda   • Go back to the sign (𝄋), then play until the measure marked *"To Coda"*, then skip to the section labelled *"Coda."*

Fill   • Label used to identify a brief pattern which is to be inserted into the arrangement.

   • Repeat measures between signs.

   • When a repeated section has different endings, play the first ending only the first time and the second ending only the second time.

Black Hole Sun

Words and Music by Chris Cornell

Drop D Tuning:
(low to high) D-A-D-G

Intro
Slow Rock ♩ = 53

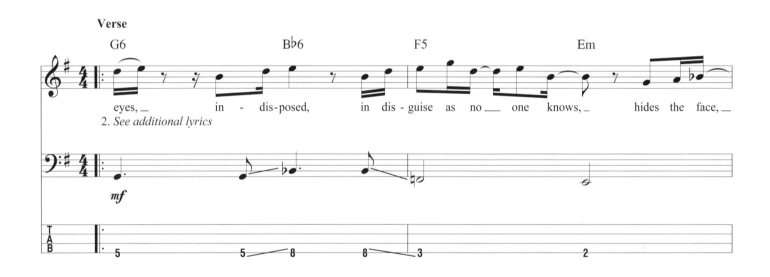

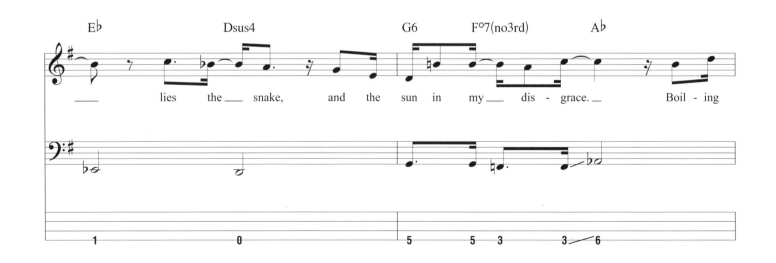

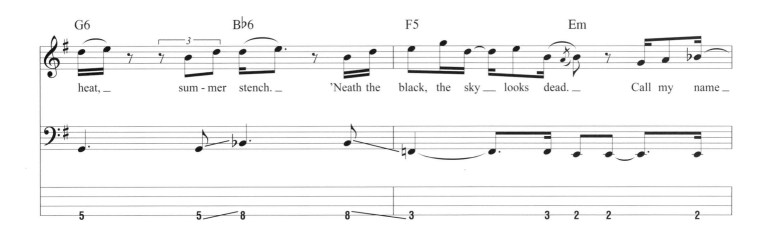

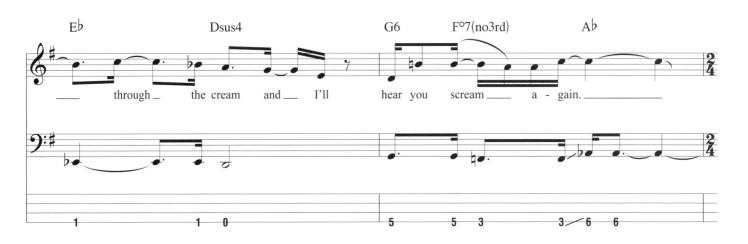

Chorus

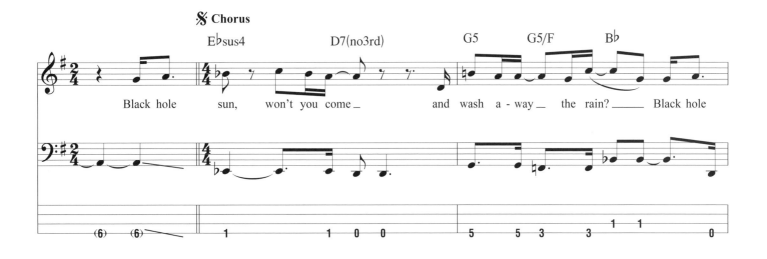

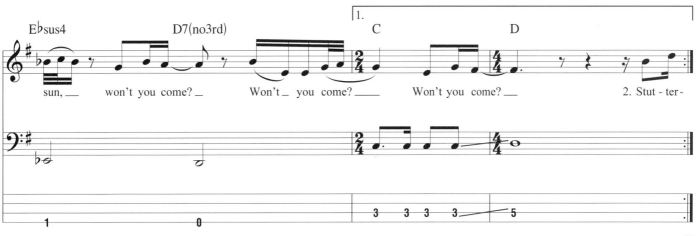

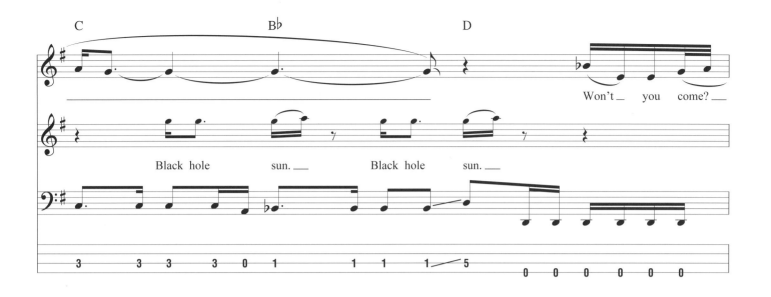

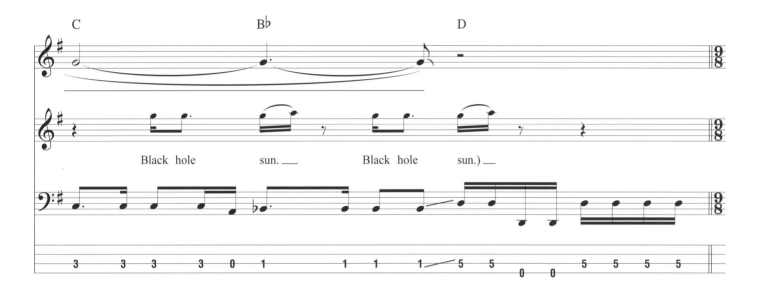

Guitar Solo

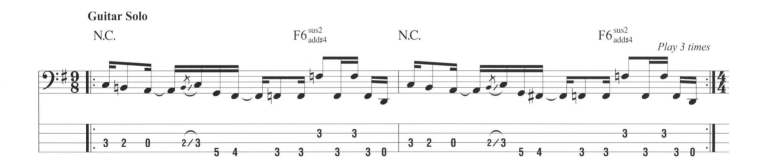

Verse

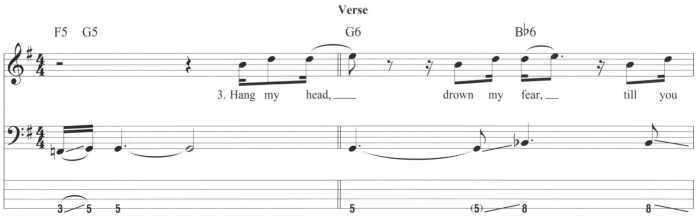

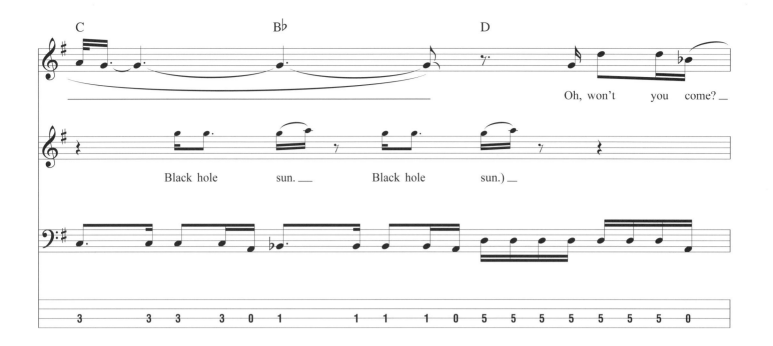

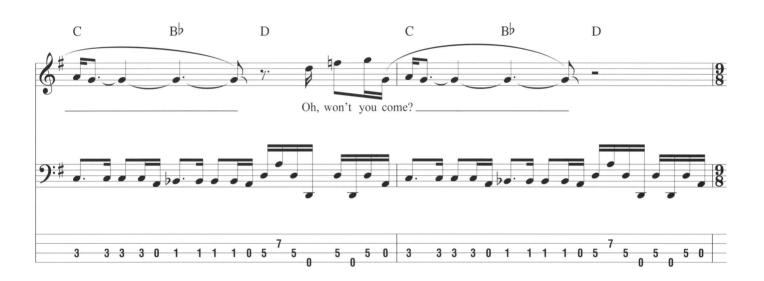

Additional Lyrics

2. Stuttering, cold and damp.
   Steal the warm wind, tired friend.
   Times are gone for honest men,
   Sometimes far too long for snakes.
   In my shoes, a walking sleep.
   In my youth I pray to keep.
   Heaven send hell away.
   No one sings like you anymore.

Buddy Holly

Words and Music by Rivers Cuomo

Tune down 1/2 step:
(low to high) Eb-Ab-Db-Gb

Verse

Moderate Rock ♩ = 120

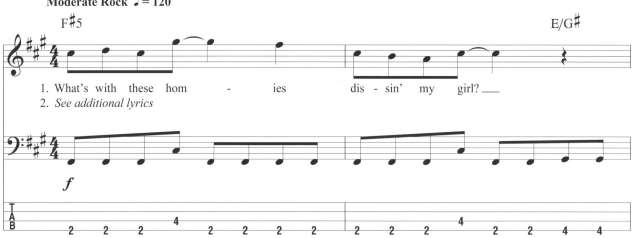

1. What's with these hom - ies dis - sin' my girl? ___
2. *See additional lyrics*

Why do they got - ta front? ___ What did we ev - er

do to these guys ___ that made them so ___ vi - o - lent?

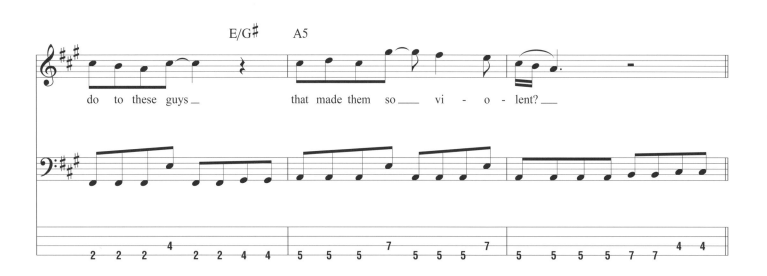

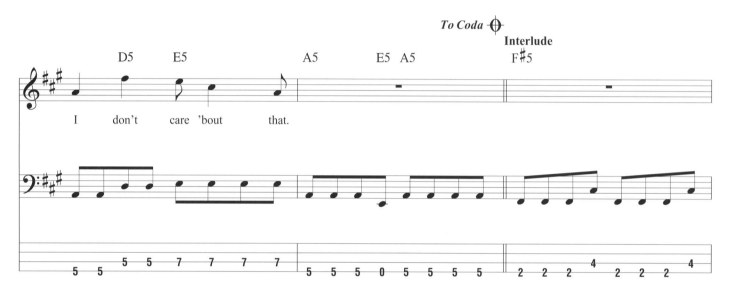

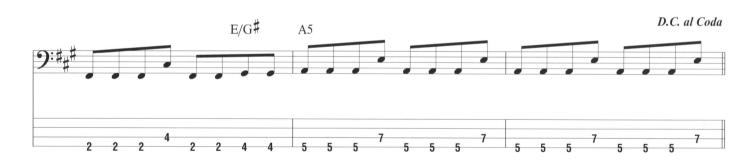

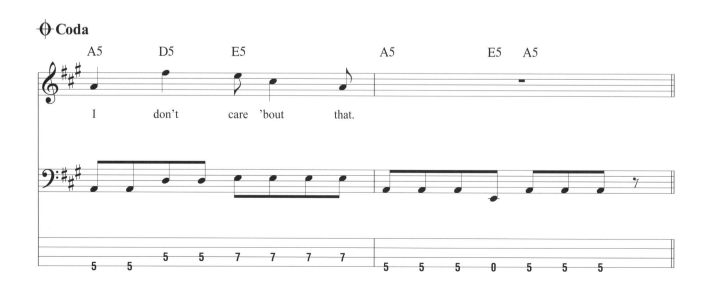

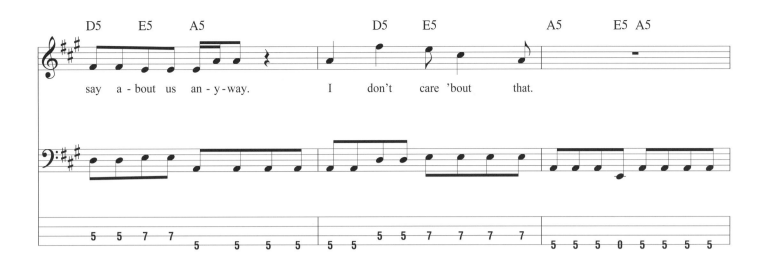

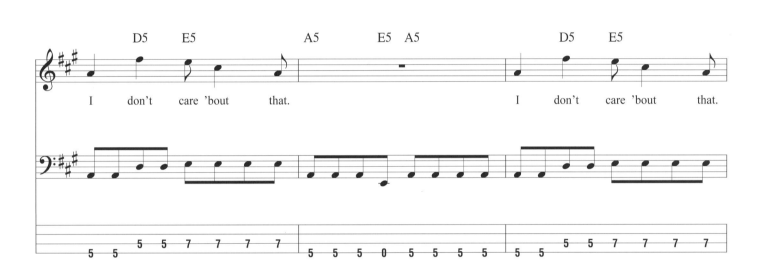

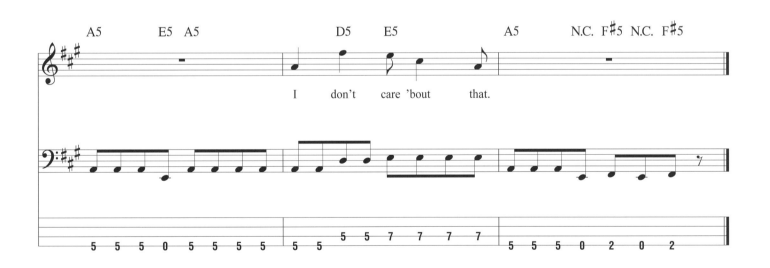

Additional Lyrics

2. Don't you ever fear, I'm always near.
   I know that you need help.
   Your tongue is twisted, your eyes are slit.
   You need a guardian.

Creep

**Words and Music by Albert Hammond, Mike Hazlewood, Thomas Yorke,
Jonathan Greenwood, Colin Greenwood, Edward O'Brien and Philip Selway**

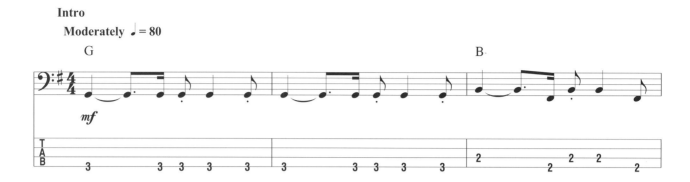

1. When you were here ___ be-fore, ___

2. *See additional lyrics*

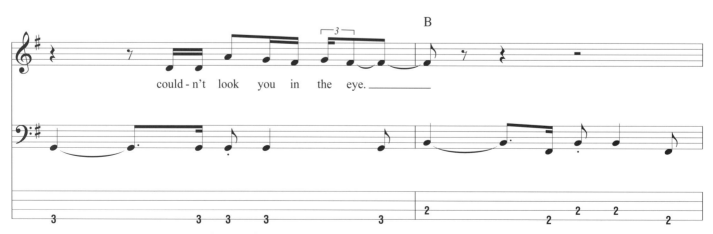

could-n't look you in the eye. ___

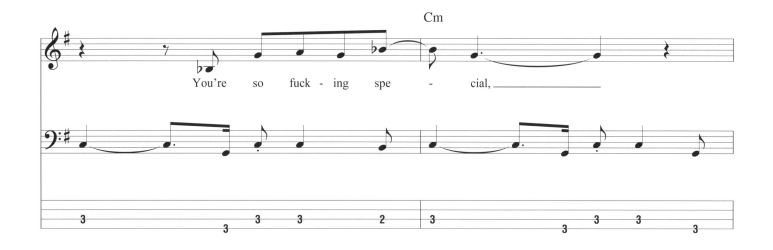

Cm

You're so fuck - ing spe - cial, _____

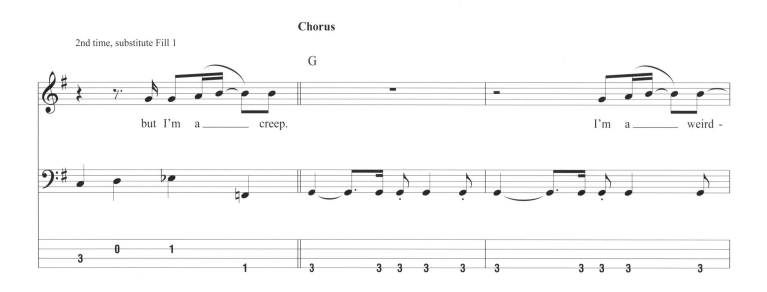

Chorus

2nd time, substitute Fill 1

G

but I'm a _____ creep. _____ I'm a _____ weird -

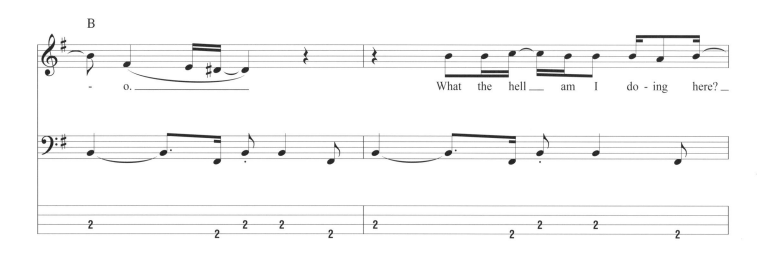

B

- o. _____ What the hell ___ am I do - ing here? ___

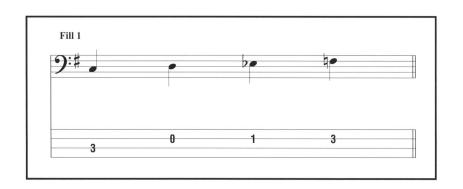

Fill 1

run, run, run, run. ____

Run. ____

Verse

3. What-ev-er makes you hap - py. What-ev-er you want. __

Additional Lyrics

2. I don't care if it hurts, I wanna have control.
I want a perfect body. I want a perfect soul.
I want you to notice when I'm not around.
You're so fucking special. I wish I was special,
But I'm a creep.

Give It Away

Words and Music by Anthony Kiedis, Flea, John Frusciante and Chad Smith

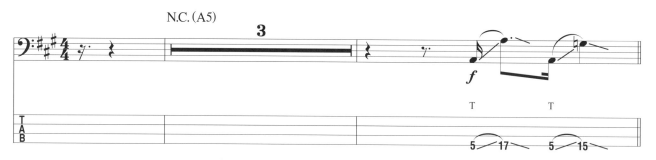

Intro
Moderate Funk ♩ = 92

N.C. (A5)

𝄋 Verse

N.C. (A5)

1., 4. What I've got, you've got to give it to your ma - ma.   What I've got, you've got to give it to your pa - pa.
2., 3. *See additional lyrics*

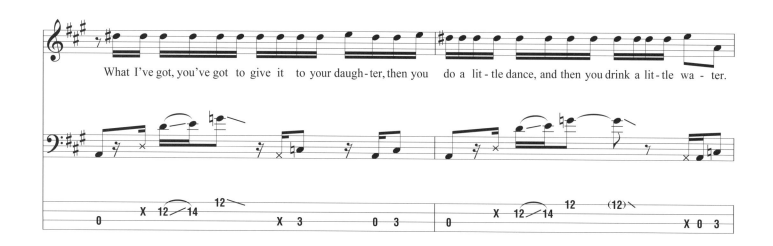

What I've got, you've got to give it to your daugh - ter, then you do a lit - tle dance, and then you drink a lit - tle wa - ter.

What I've got, you've got to get it, put it in you. What I've got, you've got to get it, put it in you.

What I've got, you've got to get it, put it in you. Reel-ing with the feel-ing, don't stop, con - tin - ue.

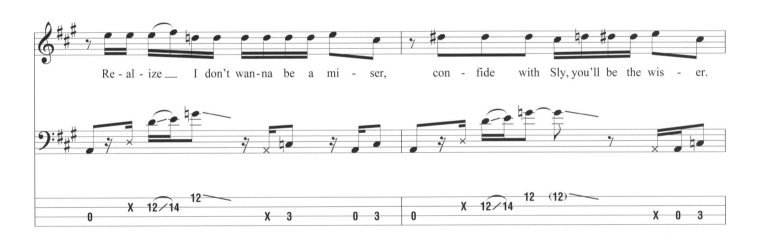

Re - al - ize___ I don't wan-na be a mi - ser, con - fide with Sly, you'll be the wis - er.

To Coda 1
To Coda 2

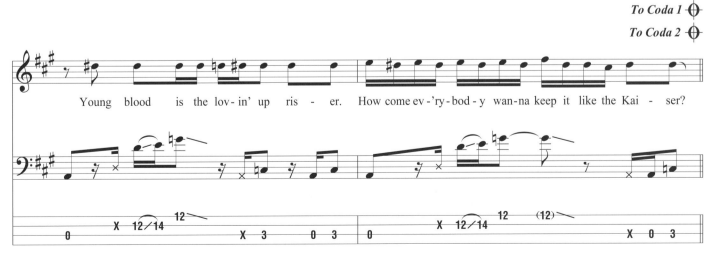

Young blood is the lov-in' up ris - er. How come ev-'ry-bod-y wan-na keep it like the Kai - ser?

Give it a-way, give it a-way, give it a-way now. __ Give it a-way, give it a-way, give it a-way now. __

Give it a-way, give it a-way, give it a-way now. __ I can't tell if I'm a king-pin or a pau-per!

Oh. Oh, yeah! __ Give it a-way, give it a-way, give it a-way now. __

Give it a-way, give it a-way, give it a-way now. __ Give it a-way, give it a-way, give it a-way now. __

Guitar Solo

N.C. (E5)

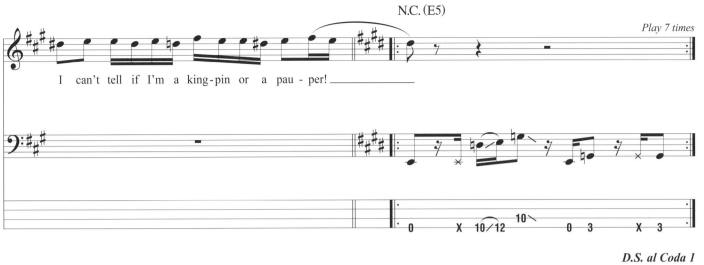

I can't tell if I'm a king-pin or a pau-per!

Play 7 times

D.S. al Coda 1

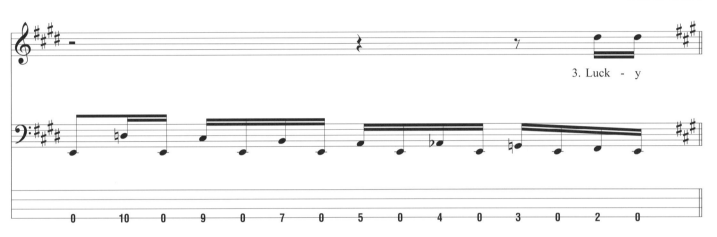

3. Luck - y

⊕ Coda 1

Chorus

N.C. (A5)

Play 3 times

Give it a-way, give it a-way, give it a-way now. _ I can't tell if I'm a king-pin or a pau-per!

*Play 1st time only.

Guitar Solo

N.C. (E5)

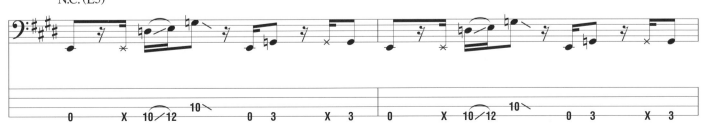

 Coda 2

Outro-Chorus

N.C. (A5)

Give it a-way,   give it a-way, give it a-way   now.___   Give it a-way,   give it a-way, give it a-way   now.___

Give it a-way,   give it a-way,   give it a-way now.___   Give it a-way,   give it a-way, give it a-way   now.___

Give it a-way now.   Give it a-way   now.

Give it a-way now.　　　　　Give it a-way now.

Give it a-way now.　　　　　Give it a-way now.

Give it a-way now.　　　　　Give it a-way now.

Give it a-way now.　　　　　Give it a-way now.

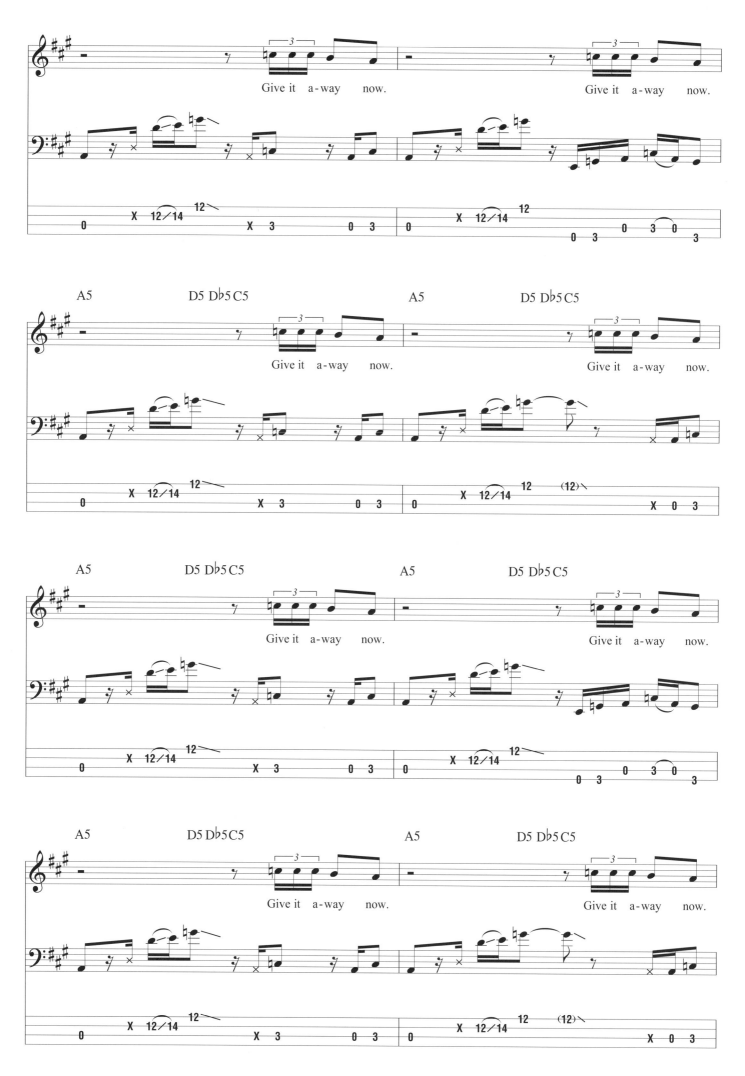

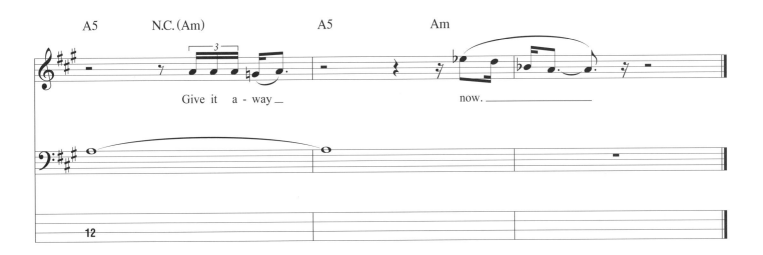

Additional Lyrics

2. Greedy little people in a sea of distress,
   Keep your move to receive your less.
   Unimpressed by material excess,
   Love is free, love me, say "Hell yes!"
   Low brow, but I rock a little know how.
   No time for the piggies or the hoosegow.
   Get smart, get down with the power,
   Never been a better time than right now.
   Bob Marley, poet and a prophet,
   Bob Marley taught me how to off it.
   Bob Marley walkin' like he talk it.
   Goodness me, can't you see I'm gonna cough it?

3. Lucky me swimmin' in my ability,
   Dancin' down on life with agility.
   Come and drink it up from my fertility,
   Blessed with a bucket of lucky mobility.
   My mom, I love her 'cause she loves me,
   Long gone are the times when she scrub me.
   Feelin' good, my brother gonna hug me,
   Drink up my juice, young love, chug-a-lug me.
   There's a river born to be a giver,
   Keep you warm, won't let you shiver.
   His heart is never gonna wither,
   Come on everybody, time to deliver.

In Bloom
Words and Music by Kurt Cobain

Intro
Moderately slow Rock ♩ = 78

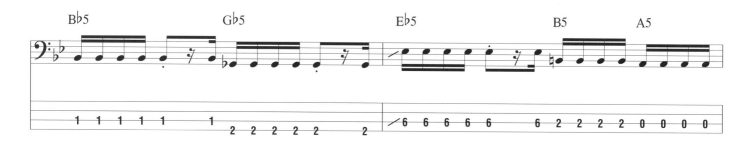

Verse

1. Sell the kids ___ for food. _____
2. *See additional lyrics*

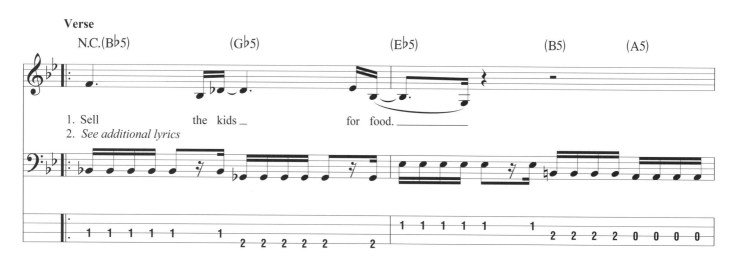

Coda

knows not   what it   means, ___   knows not   what it   means, ___

Outro

knows not   what it   means ___   and I ___ say,   "Aahh, _____

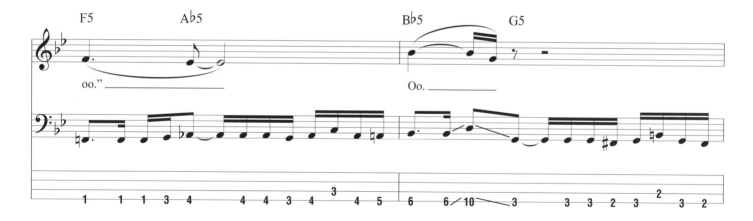

oo." _____   Oo. _____

Oo. _____

Additional Lyrics

2. We can have some more.
   Nature is a whore.
   Bruises on the fruit.
   Tender age in bloom.

Jeremy

Words by Eddie Vedder
Music by Jeff Ament

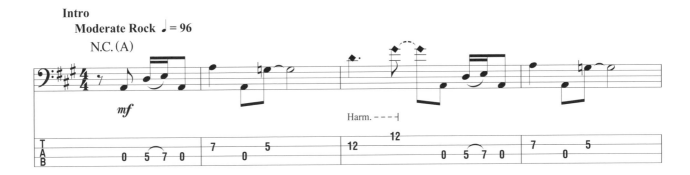

*Chords refer to gtr.

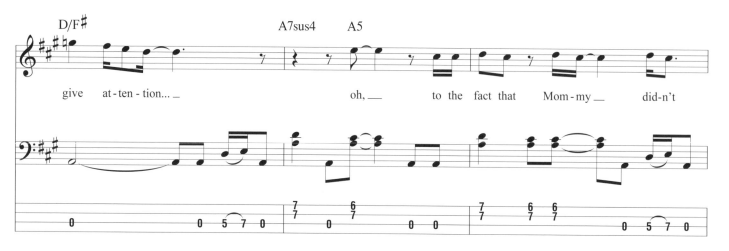

his teeth an' bit the re-cess la-dy's breast... how could I for-get... an' he hit me with a

sur-prise, left... my jaw left hurt-in'... oo, dropped wide o-pen...

just like the day... oh, like the day I heard... _

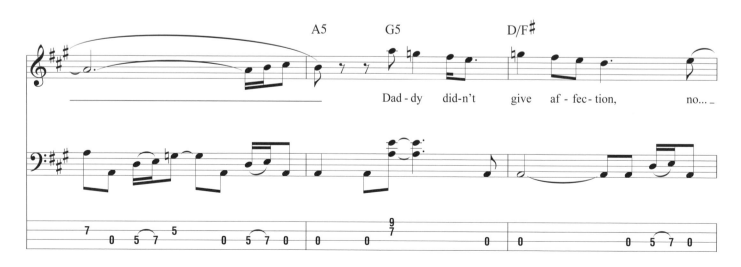

Dad-dy did-n't give af-fec-tion, no... _

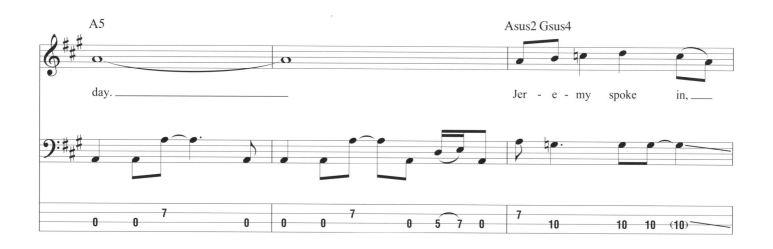

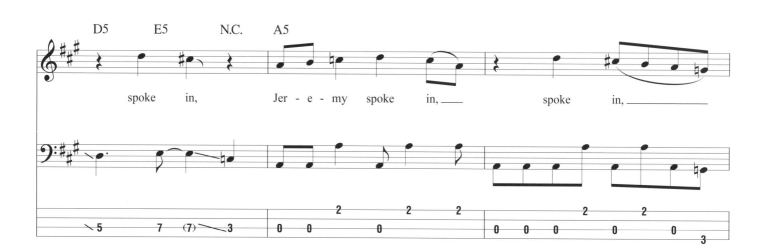

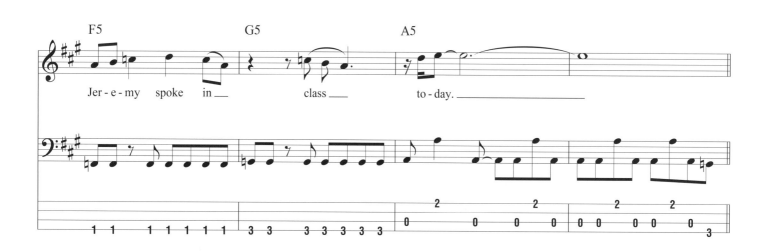

Outro

w/ Voc. ad lib., next 32 meas.

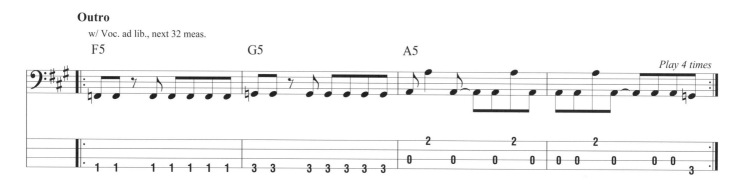

Killing in the Name

Written and Arranged by Rage Against The Machine

Drop D tuning:
(low to high) D-A-D-G

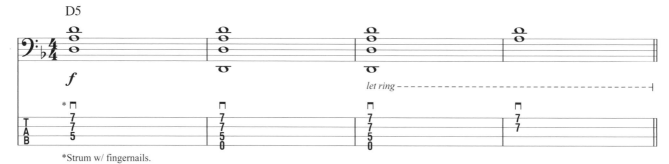

*Strum w/ fingernails.

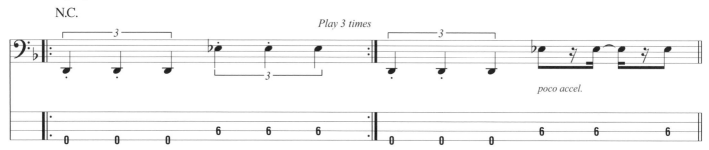

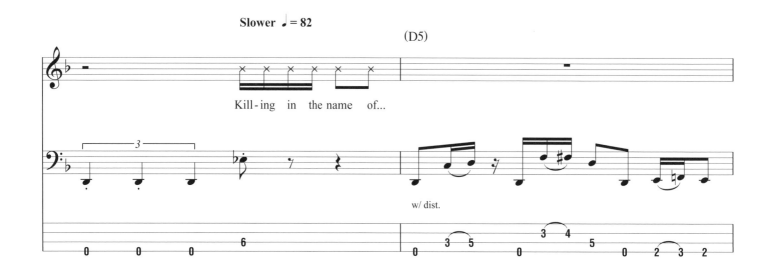

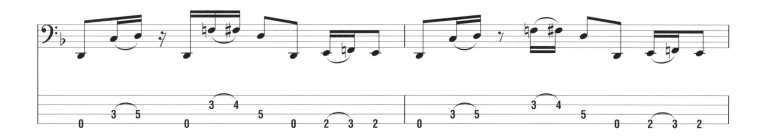

%. Verse

N.C.(D5)

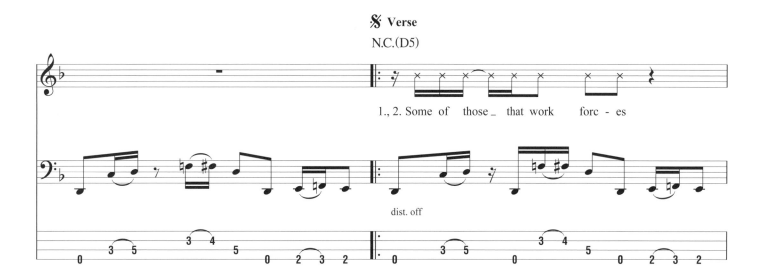

1., 2. Some of those _ that work forc - es

dist. off

Chorus

6th time, substitute Fill 1

N.C.(D5)

Play 4 times

are the same _ that burn cross - es.

Uh.

Play 4 times

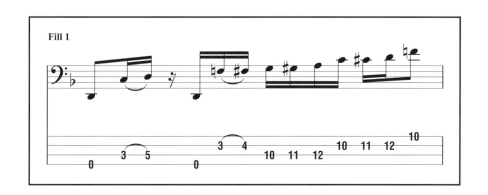

Fill 1

2nd time, D.S. al Coda

Coda

Interlude

Faster ♩ = 90

wear-ing your badge _ and your cho - sen white. You'll jus - ti - fy ___ those {that/who} died _ by

wear-ing a badge _ and your chos - en white.

N.C.(D5)

Play 4 times

And now you do what they told _ ya.

Play 4 times

Slightly faster ♩ = 93

Play 6 times

And now you do what they told _ ya.
And now you're un-der con-trol.

And now you do what they told _ ya.
And now you're

Play 6 times

Slightly slower ♩ = 89

But now you do what they told _ ya.
un-der con-trol. ___

Those who died _ are jus - ti - fied _ by

wear-ing your badge _ and your cho - sen white. You'll jus - ti - fy _ those that died _ by

1.
wear-ing a badge _ and your chos - en white.

2.
wear-ing a badge _ and your chos - en white. Come on! _

Guitar Solo

N.C.(D5)

Uh!

Yeah.

You Oughta Know

Lyrics by Alanis Morissette
Music by Alanis Morissette and Glen Ballard

Tune down 1/2 step:
(low to high) Eb-Ab-Db-Gb

Verse
Moderately ♩ = 106

N.C.

1. I want you ___ to know that I'm hap - py ___ for you.

I wish noth - ing but the best ___ for ___ you both. An old - er

ver - sion of me, is she per - vert - ed like _ me? Would she go down on you in ___ a the-a-

Gm7

tre? Does she speak el - o - quent - ly, and would she

Interlude

Bass tacet

C7sus4 ... C7

C7sus4 ... C7

Ah. ... Ah.

Gm/C ... C

Ah. ... Ah.

C7 ... Gm/C

Ah. ___ Ah. ___ Ah. ___ Ah. ___ Ah. ___ 'Cause the

Pre-Chorus

Gm7

joke that you laid in the bed, that was me and I'm not gon-na fade as soon as you close

Bass

mf

C/G

your eyes, and you __ know it. And ev -

HAL•LEONARD® BASS PLAY-ALONG

AUDIO ACCESS INCLUDED

The Bass Play-Along™ Series will help you play your favorite songs quickly and easily! Just follow the tab, listen to the audio to hear how the bass should sound, and then play-along using the separate backing tracks. The melody and lyrics are also included in the book in case you want to sing, or to simply help you follow along. The audio files are enhanced so you can adjust the recording to any tempo without changing pitch!

1. Rock
00699674 ....$15.99

2. R&B
00699675 ....$15.99

3. Pop/Rock
00699677 ....$16.99

5. Funk
00699680 ....$16.99

6. Classic Rock
00699678 ....$16.99

7. Hard Rock
00699676 ....$16.99

9. Blues
00699817 ....$16.99

10. Jimi Hendrix Smash Hits
00699815 ....$17.99

11. Country
00699818 ....$12.95

12. Punk Classics
00699814 ....$12.99

13. The Beatles
00275504 ....$16.99

14. Modern Rock
00699821 ....$14.99

15. Mainstream Rock
00699822 ....$14.99

16. '80s Metal
00699825 ....$16.99

17. Pop Metal
00699826 ....$14.99

18. Blues Rock
00699828 ....$14.99

19. Steely Dan
00700203 ....$16.99

20. The Police
00700270 ....$17.99

21. Metallica: 1983-1988
00234338 ....$19.99

22. Metallica: 1991-2016
00234339 ....$19.99

**23. Pink Floyd –
Dark Side of The Moon**
00700847 ....$15.99

24. Weezer
00700960 ....$14.99

25. Nirvana
00701047 ....$15.99

26. Black Sabbath
00701180 ....$16.99

27. Kiss
00701181 ....$16.99

28. The Who
00701182 ....$16.99

29. Eric Clapton
00701183 ....$15.99

30. Early Rock
00701184 ....$15.99

31. The 1970s
00701185 ....$14.99

32. Cover Band Hits
00211598 ....$16.99

33. Christmas Hits
00701197 ....$12.99

34. Easy Songs
00701480 ....$16.99

35. Bob Marley
00701702 ....$17.99

36. Aerosmith
00701886 ....$14.99

37. Modern Worship
00701920 ....$14.99

38. Avenged Sevenfold
00702386 ....$16.99

40. AC/DC
14041594 ....$16.99

41. U2
00702582 ....$16.99

42. Red Hot Chili Peppers
00702991 ....$19.99

43. Paul McCartney
00703079 ....$17.99

44. Megadeth
00703080 ....$16.99

45. Slipknot
00703201 ....$16.99

46. Best Bass Lines Ever
00103359 ....$19.99

47. Dream Theater
00111940 ....$24.99

48. James Brown
00117421 ....$16.99

49. Eagles
00119936 ....$17.99

50. Jaco Pastorius
00128407 ....$17.99

51. Stevie Ray Vaughan
00146154 ....$16.99

52. Cream
00146159 ....$17.99

56. Bob Seger
00275503 ....$16.99

57. Iron Maiden
00278398 ....$17.99

58. Southern Rock
00278436 ....$17.99

HAL•LEONARD®

Prices, contents, and availability subject to change without notice.

Visit Hal Leonard Online at **www.halleonard.com**

BASS RECORDED VERSIONS

Bass Recorded Versions feature authentic transcriptions written in standard notation and tablature for bass guitar. This series features complete bass lines from the classics to contemporary superstars.

**25 Essential
Rock Bass Classics**
00690210 / $17.99

**Avenged Sevenfold –
Nightmare**
00691054 / $19.99

Bass Tab White Pages
00690508 / $29.99

The Beatles – Abbey Road
00128336 / $22.99

The Beatles Bass Lines
00690170 / $14.95

The Beatles 1962-1966
00690556 / $19.99

The Beatles 1967-1970
00690557 / $22.99

The Best of Blink 182
00690549 / $18.95

Best of Bass Tab
00141806 / $15.99

Blues Bass Classics
00690291 / $17.99

Boston Bass Collection
00690935 / $19.95

Stanley Clarke Collection
00672307 / $19.99

**Dream Theater
Bass Anthology**
00119345 / $24.99

Funk Bass Bible
00690744 / $24.99

Hard Rock Bass Bible
00690746 / $19.99

**Jimi Hendrix –
Are You Experienced?**
00690371 / $17.95

**Jimi Hendrix Bass
Tab Collection**
00160505 / $22.99

**Iron Maiden Bass
Anthology**
00690867 / $22.99

Jazz Bass Classics
00102070 / $17.99

Best of Kiss for Bass
00690080 / $19.95

**Lynyrd Skynyrd –
All-Time Greatest Hits**
00690956 / $19.99

Bob Marley Bass Collection
00690568 / $19.99

Mastodon – Crack the Skye
00691007 / $19.99

Megadeth Bass Anthology
00691191 / $19.99

Metal Bass Tabs
00103358 / $19.99

Best of Marcus Miller
00690811 / $24.99

Motown Bass Classics
00690253 / $16.99

Muse Bass Tab Collection
00123275 / $19.99

Nirvana Bass Collection
00690066 / $19.99

No Doubt – Tragic Kingdom
00120112 / $22.95

**The Offspring –
Greatest Hits**
00690809 / $17.95

**Jaco Pastorius –
Greatest Jazz Fusion
Bass Player**
00690421 / $19.99

The Essential Jaco Pastorius
00690420 / $19.99

Pearl Jam – Ten
00694882 / $17.99

**Pink Floyd –
Dark Side of the Moon**
00660172 / $15.99

The Best of Police
00660207 / $19.99

Pop/Rock Bass Bible
00690747 / $17.95

Queen – The Bass Collection
00690065 / $19.99

R&B Bass Bible
00690745 / $22.99

Rage Against the Machine
00690248 / $19.99

**The Best of
Red Hot Chili Peppers**
00695285 / $24.99

**Red Hot Chili Peppers –
Blood Sugar Sex Magik**
00690064 / $19.99

**Red Hot Chili Peppers –
By the Way**
00690585 / $22.99

**Red Hot Chili Peppers –
Californication**
00690390 / $19.99

**Red Hot Chili Peppers –
Greatest Hits**
00690675 / $19.99

**Red Hot Chili Peppers –
I'm with You**
00691167 / $22.99

**Red Hot Chili Peppers –
One Hot Minute**
00690091 / $19.99

**Red Hot Chili Peppers –
Stadium Arcadium**
00690853 / $24.95

**Red Hot Chili Peppers –
Stadium Arcadium**
00690853 / $24.95

Rock Bass Bible
00690446 / $19.99

Rolling Stones
00690256 / $17.99

Royal Blood
00151826 / $22.99

Slap Bass Bible
00159716 / $24.99

**Sly & The Family Stone
for Bass**
00109733 / $19.99

Best of Billy Sheehan
00173972 / $24.99

Best of Yes
00103044 / $19.99

Best of ZZ Top for Bass
00691069 / $22.99

Visit Hal Leonard Online at
www.halleonard.com

BUILD UP YOUR BASS CHOPS

100 FUNK/R&B LESSONS

Expand your bass knowledge with the Bass Lesson Goldmine series! Featuring 100 individual modules covering a giant array of topics, each lesson in this Funk/R&B volume includes detailed instruction with playing examples presented in standard notation and tablature. You'll also get extremely useful tips, scale diagrams, chord grids, photos, and more to reinforce your learning experience plus audio tracks featuring performance demos of all the examples in the book!

00131463 Book/Online Audio $24.99

BASS AEROBICS
by Jon Liebman

A 52-week, one-exercise-per-week workout program for developing, improving, and maintaining bass guitar technique. This book/CD will benefit all levels of players, from beginners to advanced, in all musical styles. The CD includes demos as well as play-along grooves. By using this program you'll increase your speed, improve your dexterity and accuracy, heighten your coordination, and increase your groove vocabulary!

00696437 Book/Online Audio $19.99

BASS FRETBOARD ATLAS
by Joe Charupakorn

Mastering the bass neck has always been a challenge, even for very experienced players. The diagrams in *Bass Fretboard Atlas* will help you quickly memorize scales and arpeggios that may have previously seemed impossible to grasp. You'll be able to easily see and understand how scale and arpeggio shapes are laid out and how they connect and overlap across the neck.

00201827 .... $19.99

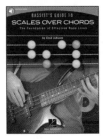

BASSIST'S GUIDE TO SCALES OVER CHORDS
by Chad Johnson

With *Bassist's Guide to Scales Over Chords*, you'll learn how these two topics are intertwined in a logical and fundamental manner. This key concept is paramount in learning how to create and improvise functional and memorable bass lines or solos reliably time and again. This book includes 136 audio tracks and 17 extended backing tracks for download or streaming online.

00151930 Book/Online Audio $19.99

FRETBOARD ROADMAPS – BASS
by Fred Sokolow & Tim Emmons

This book/audio pack will get you playing bass lines anywhere on the fretboard, in any key. You'll learn to build bass lines under chord progressions; major, minor, and pentatonic scale patterns; and much more through easy-to-follow diagrams and instructions for beginning, intermediate, and advanced players. The online audio includes 64 demonstration and play-along tracks.

00695840 Book/Online Audio $17.99

LOUIS JOHNSON – BASS MASTER CLASS

For the first time, the legendary Louis Johnson "Star Licks" bass instruction videos are being made available in book format with online access to all the classic video footage. This package compiles Volumes I and II of the original Star Licks Master Classes into one bundle, giving you over an hour and a half of instruction, while the book contains transcriptions of every example played! All music is written in both standard notation and tab.

00156138 Book with Online Video $19.99

MUSIC THEORY FOR BASS PLAYERS
by Steve Gorenberg

With this comprehensive workbook, you'll expand your fretboard knowledge and gain the freedom and confidence needed to tackle any musical challenge. Features hundreds of examples to study and practice, including loads of "real world" bass lines and play-along audio tracks to jam to! Includes over 200 demonstration and play-along audio tracks and three bass fretboard theory video lessons online for download or streaming.

00197904 Book/Online Media $24.99

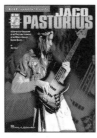

JACO PASTORIUS – BASS SIGNATURE LICKS
by Dan Towey

Learn the trademark grooves and solos of the man who revolutionized bass guitar. This book/CD pack will help you take a closer look at Jaco's rich body of work through the structural, theoretical, and harmonic analysis of these classic recordings: Birdland • Bright Size Life • Come On, Come Over • Continuum • Donna Lee • God Must Be a Boogie Man • Kuru • Liberty City • Night Passage • Palladium • Port of Entry • Portrait of Tracy • Rockin' in Rhythm • Talk to Me • Teen Town.

00695544 Book/CD Pack................................... $24.95

PLAY LIKE JACO PASTORIUS
THE ULTIMATE BASS LESSON
by Jon Liebman

Study the trademark songs, licks, tones and techniques of the world's greatest jazz fusion bassist, Jaco Pastorius. This comprehensive book/audio teaching method provides detailed analysis of Pastorius' gear, techniques, styles, songs, riffs and more. Each book comes with a unique code that will give you access to audio files of all the music in the book online. This pack looks at 15 of Jaco's most influential songs.

00128409 Book/Online Audio $19.99

STUFF! GOOD BASS PLAYERS SHOULD KNOW
by Glenn Letsch

Provides valuable tips on performing, recording, the music business, instruments and equipment (including electronics), grooves, fills, soloing techniques, care & maintenance, and more. Covers rock, jazz, blues, R&B and funk through demos of authentic grooves. The accompanying recordings include many of the examples in the book performed both in solo bass format and in a full-band setting so you can hear how important concepts fit in with other instruments and ensembles.

00696014 Book/Online Audio $19.99

WARM-UP EXERCISES FOR BASS GUITAR
by Steve Gorenberg

Bass players: customize your warm-up routine with this fantastic collection of stretches, coordination exercises, pentatonic scales, major and minor scales, and arpeggios sure to limber up your fingers and hands and get you ready to play in top form!

00148760 .... $9.99

HAL•LEONARD®
www.halleonard.com

View our website for hundreds more bass books!

Prices, contents, and availability subject to change without notice.